VAGINARAMA
A SPECIAL VAGINA COLORING BOOK
BY MASSIMO WOLKE

VAGINARAMA
A SPECIAL VAGINA COLORING BOOK
BY MASSIMO WOLKE

Bibliografische Information der Deutschen Nationalbibliothek:
Die Deutsche Nationalbibliothek verzeichnet diese Publikation in der
Deutschen Nationalbibliografie; detaillierte bibliografische Daten sind
im Internet über http://dnb.dnb.de abrufbar.

Herstellung und Verlag:
BoD - Books on Demand, Norderstedt

ISBN: 978-3-7528-1991-5

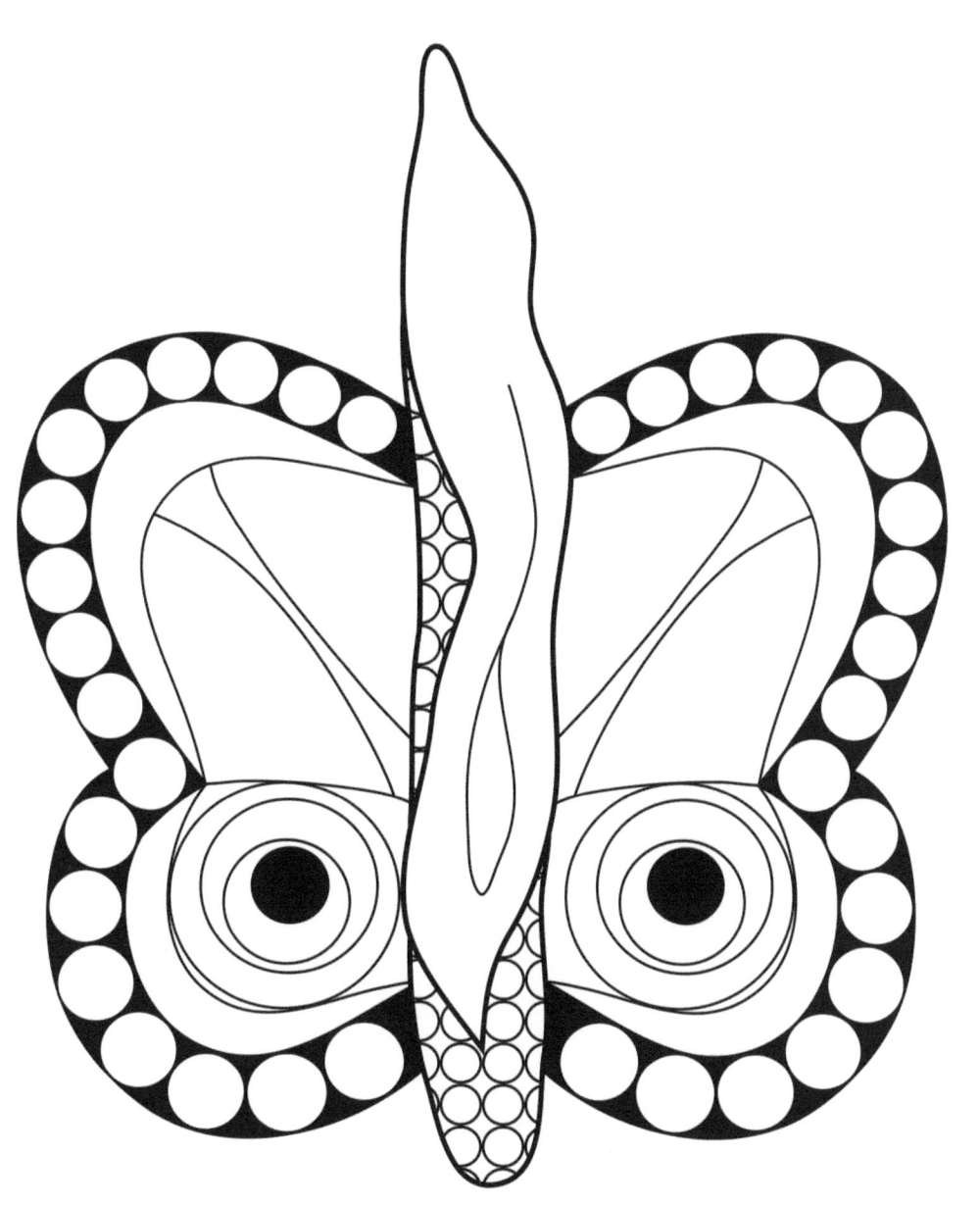

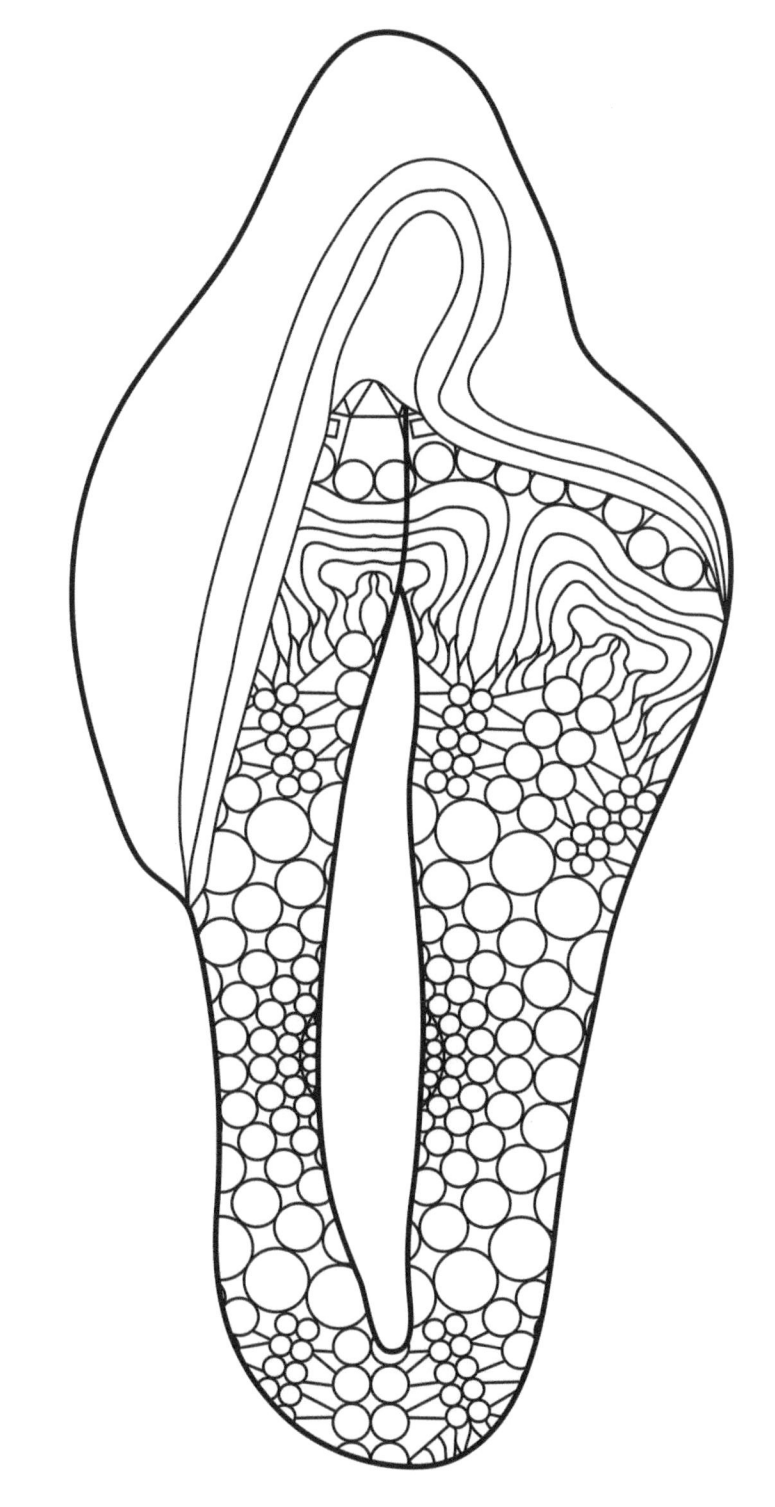

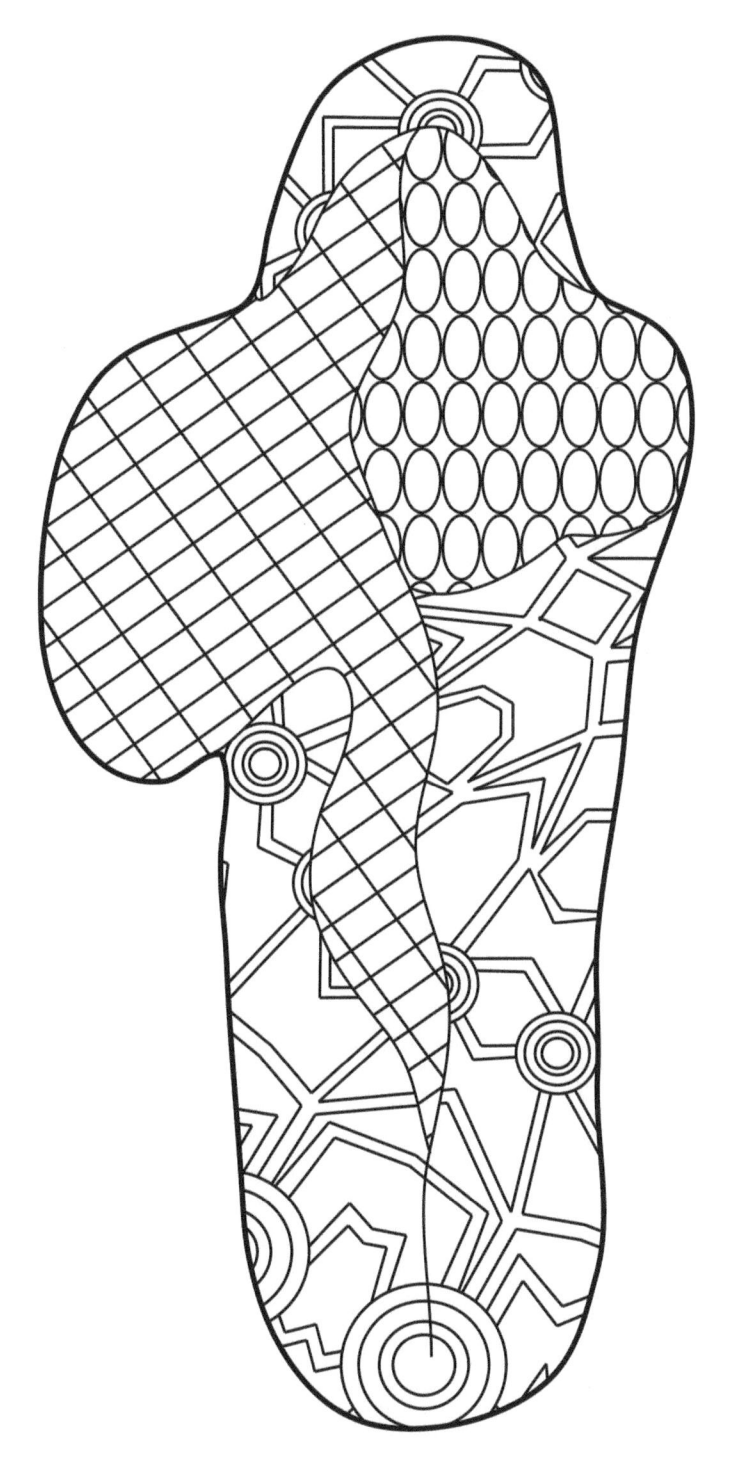

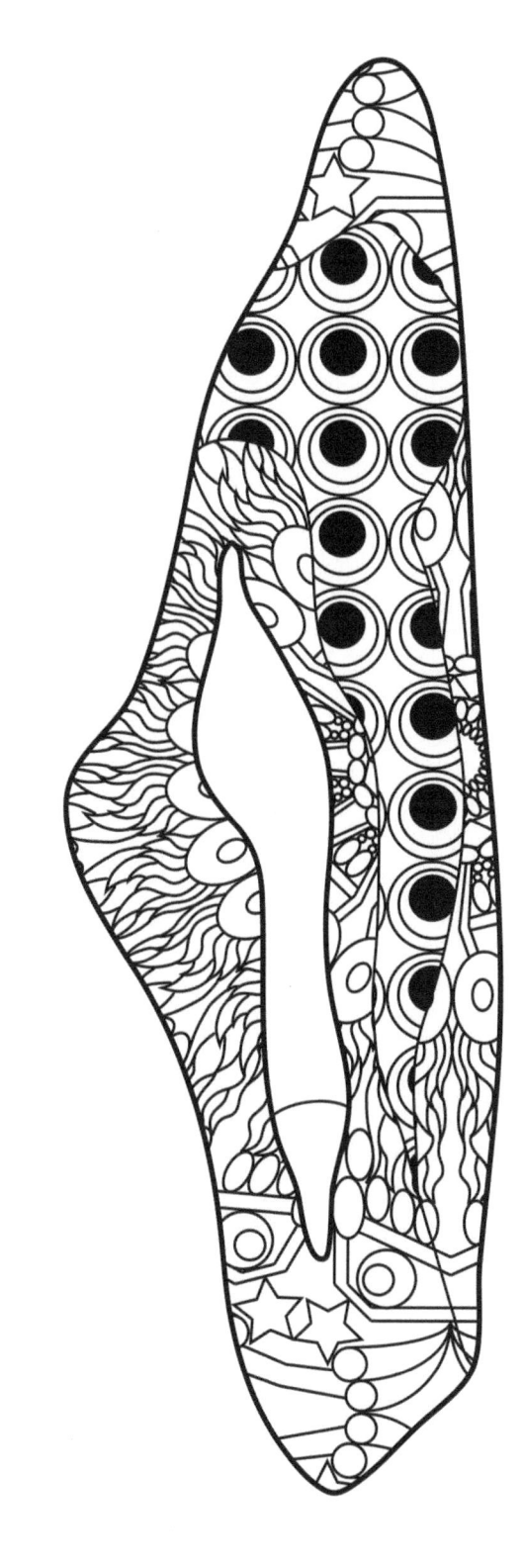

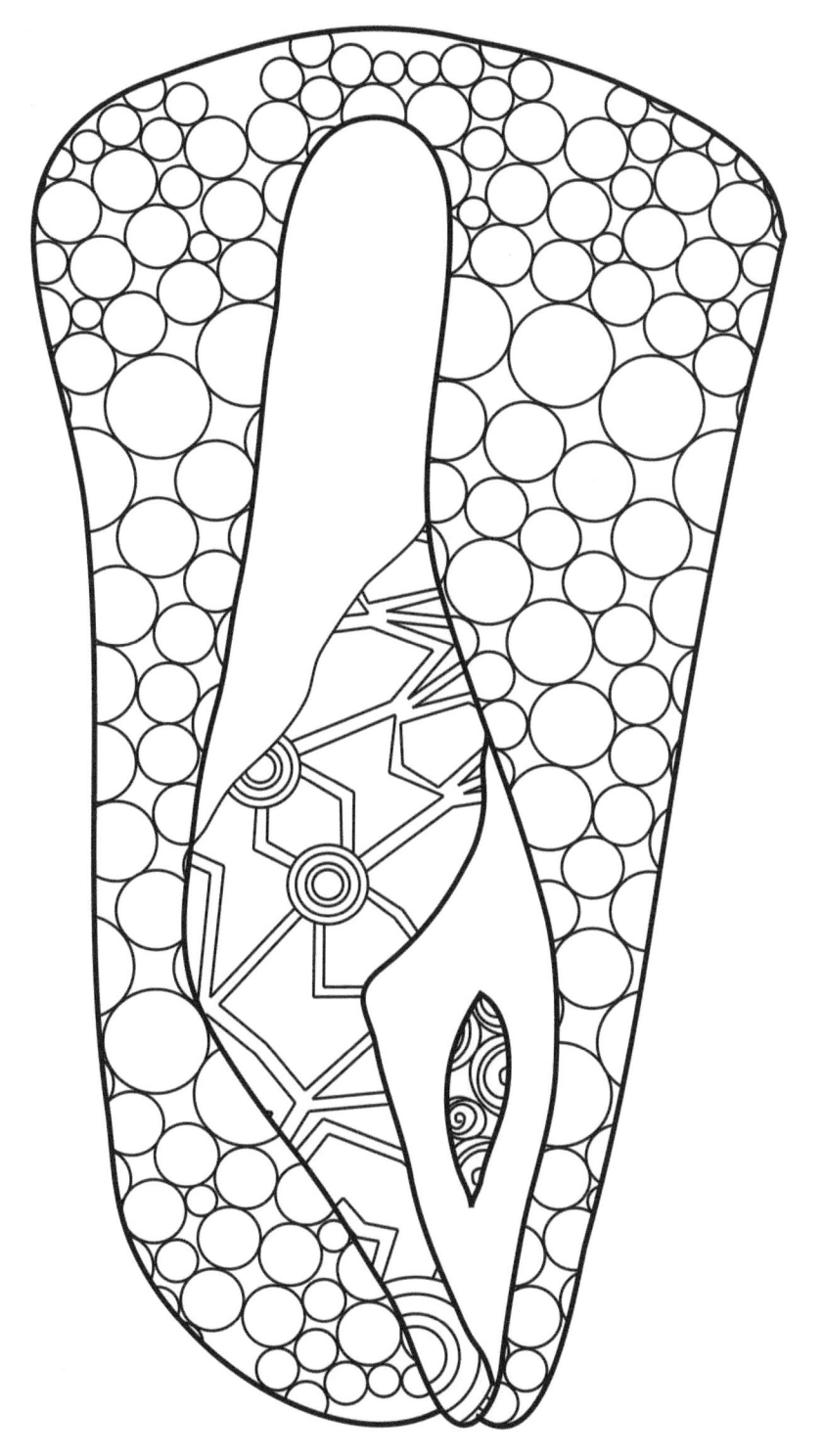

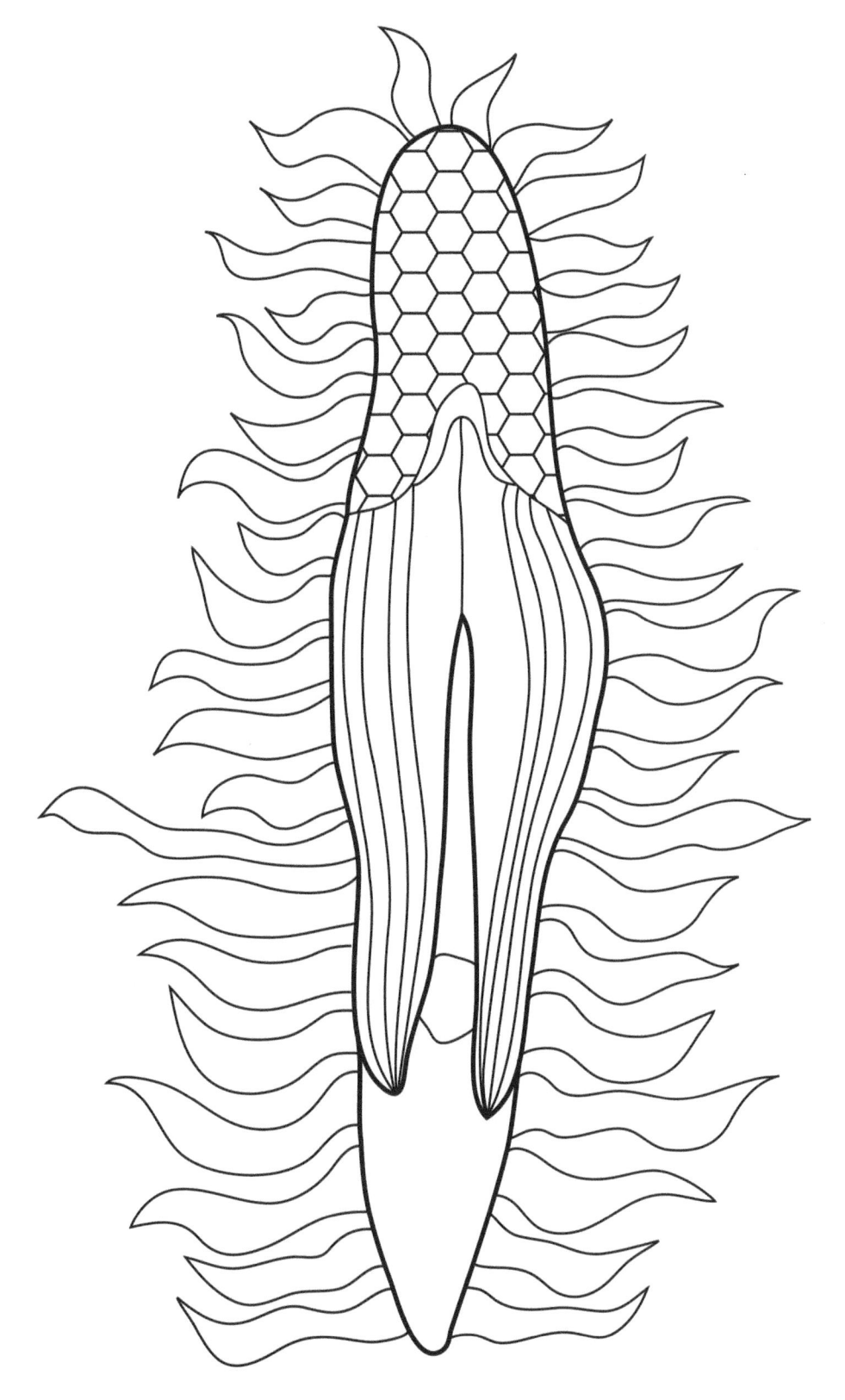

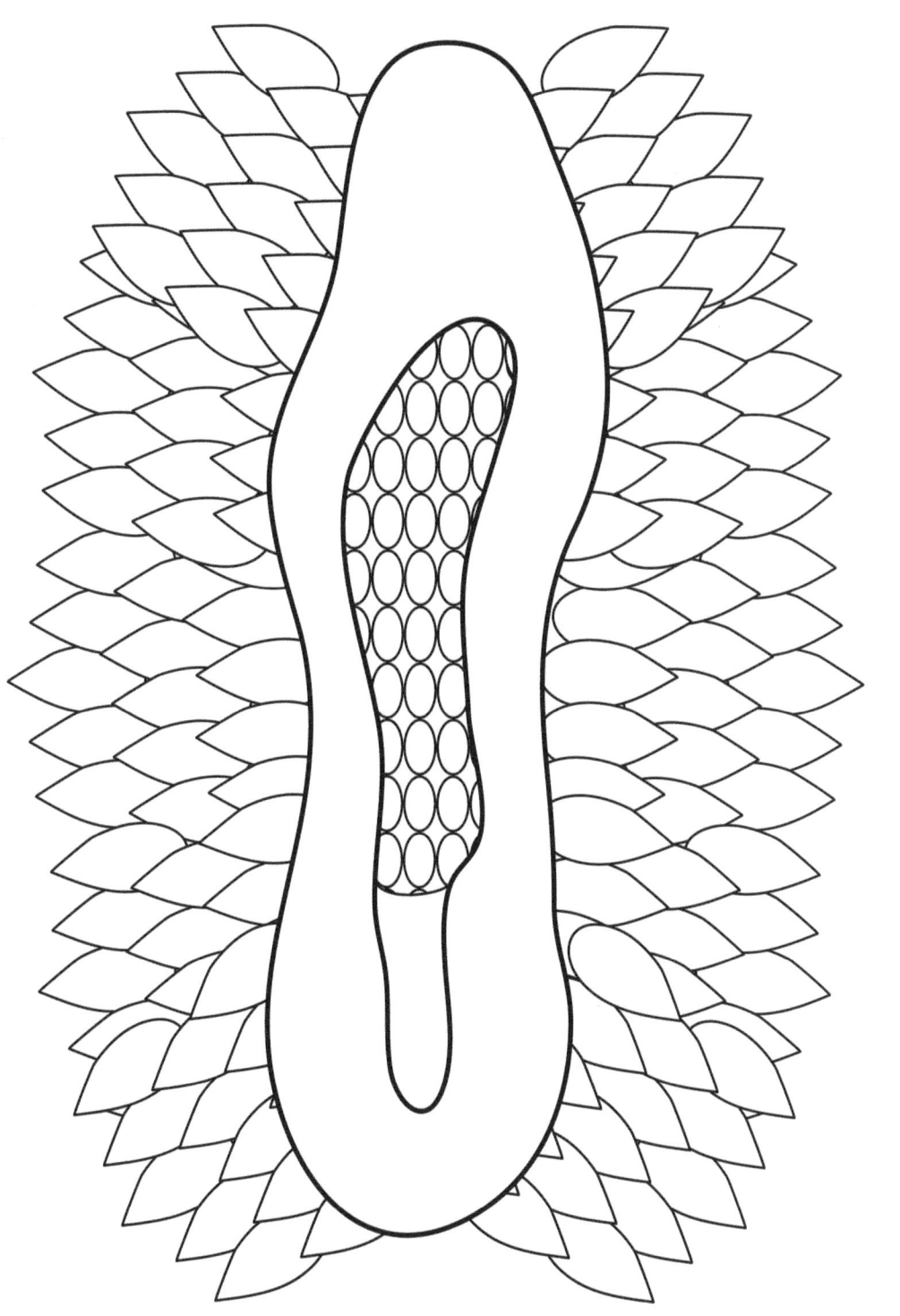

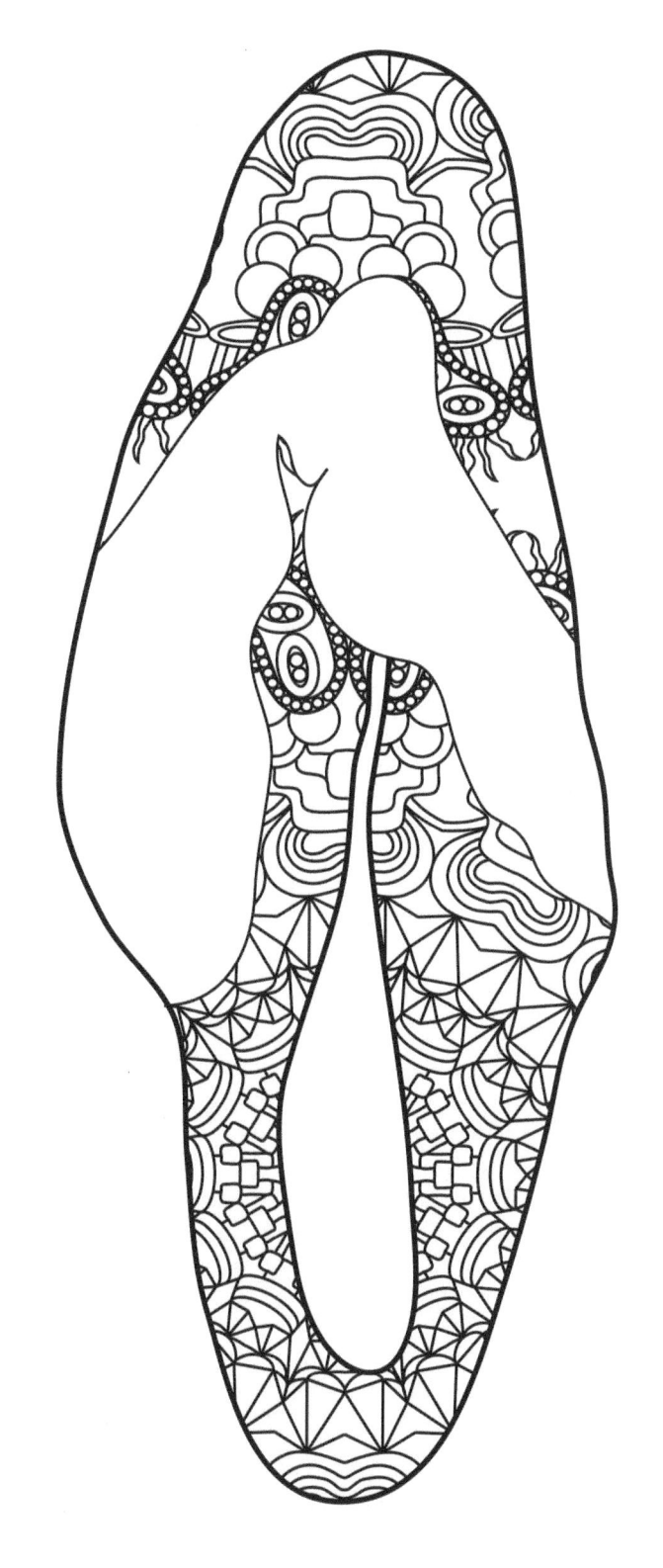

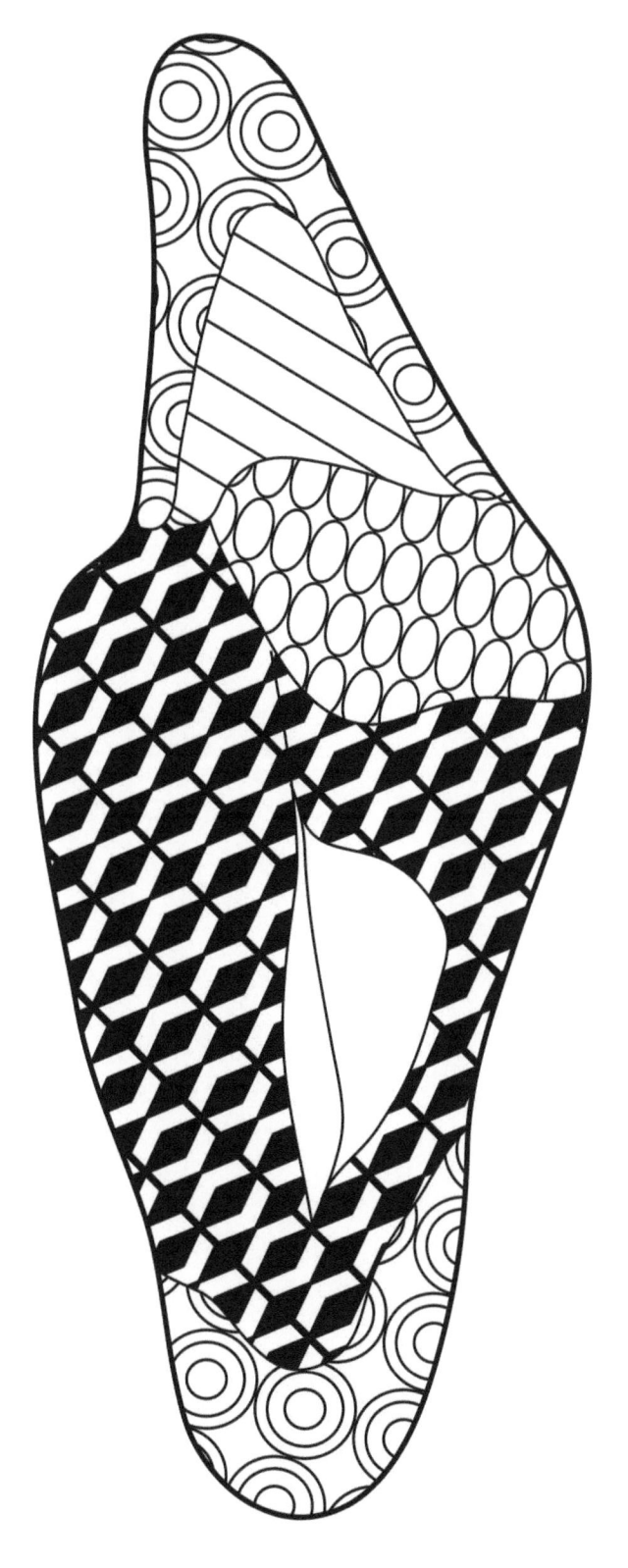

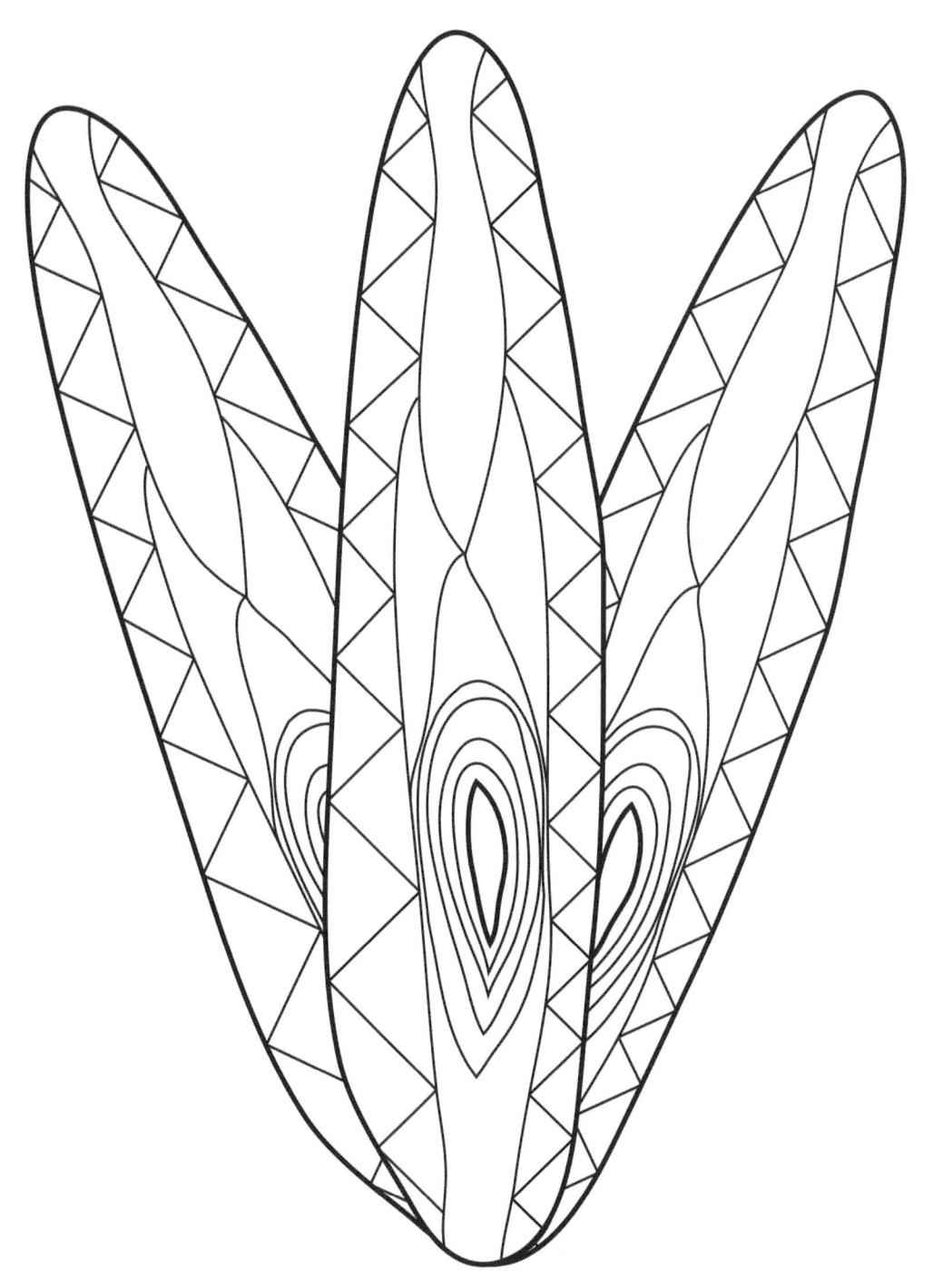

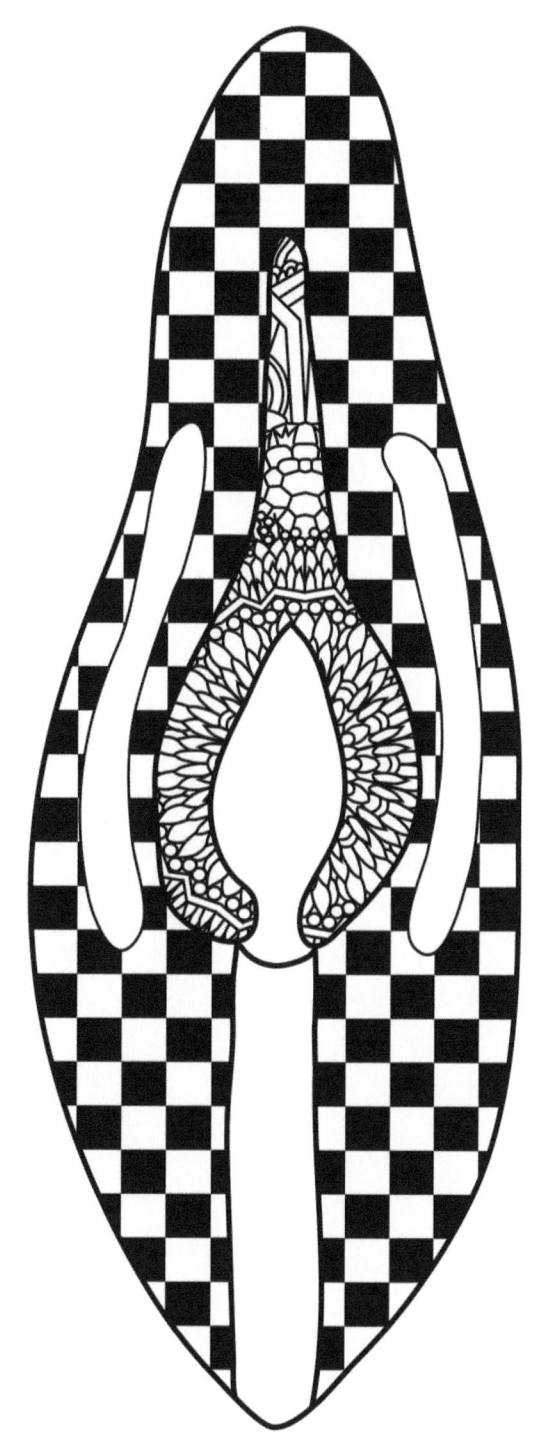

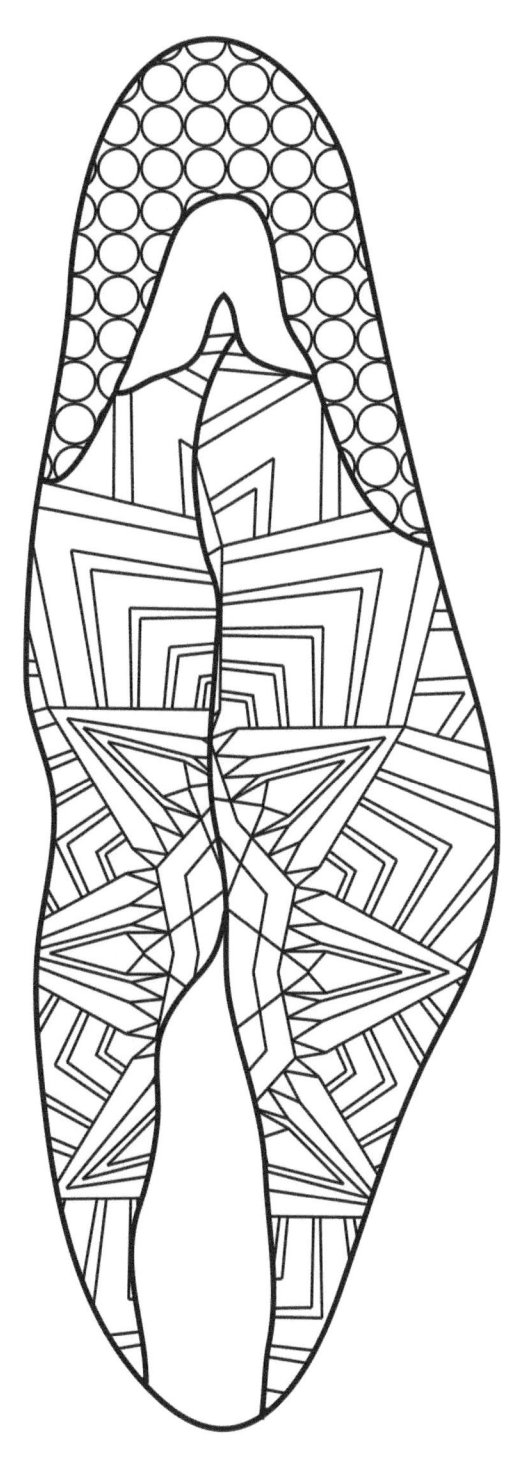

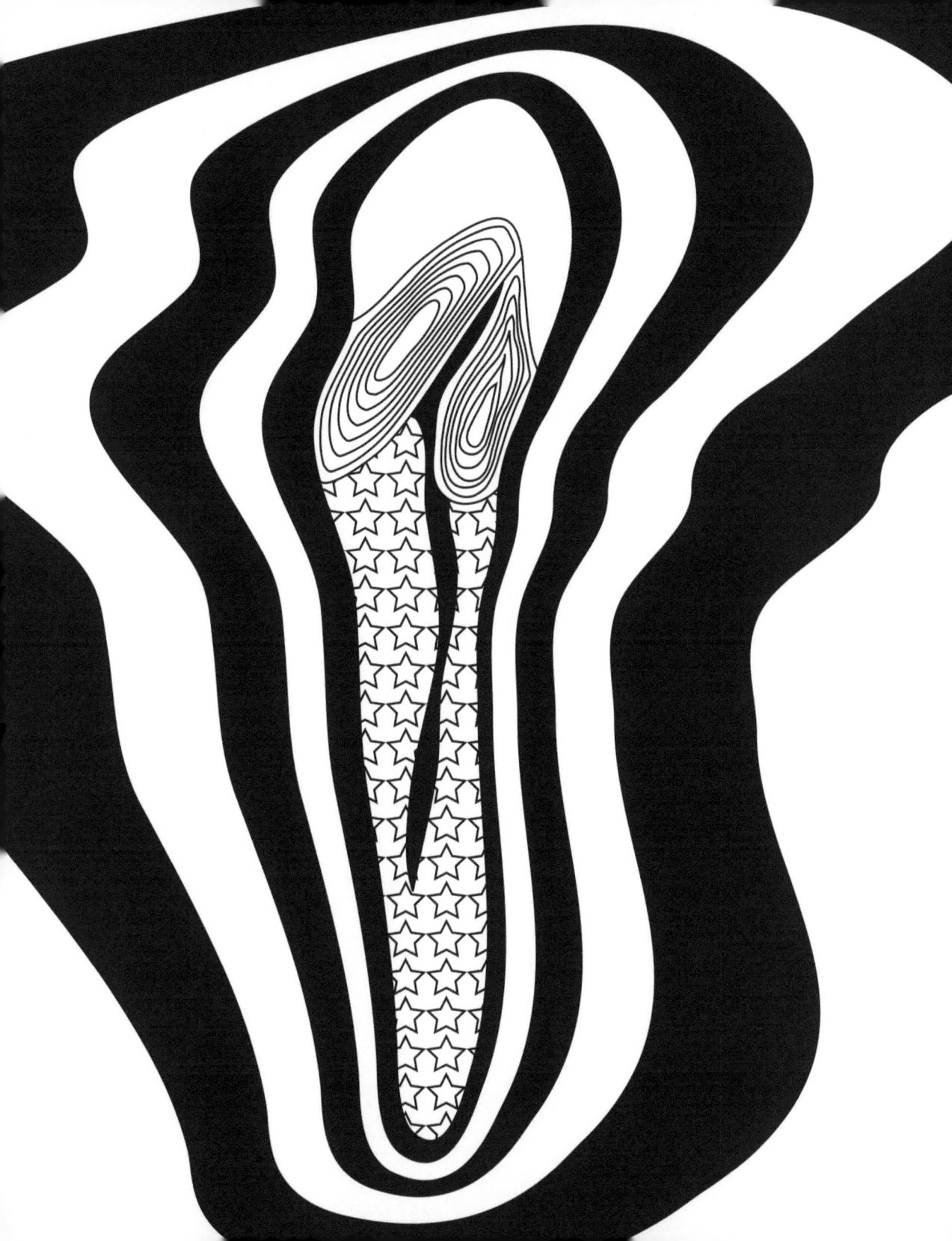

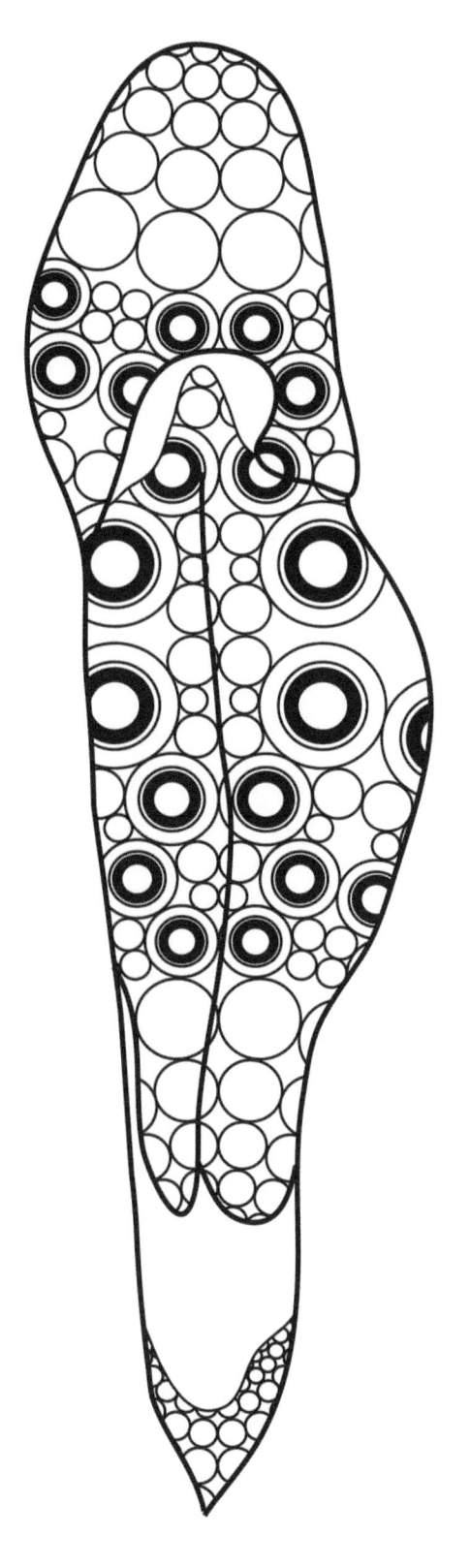

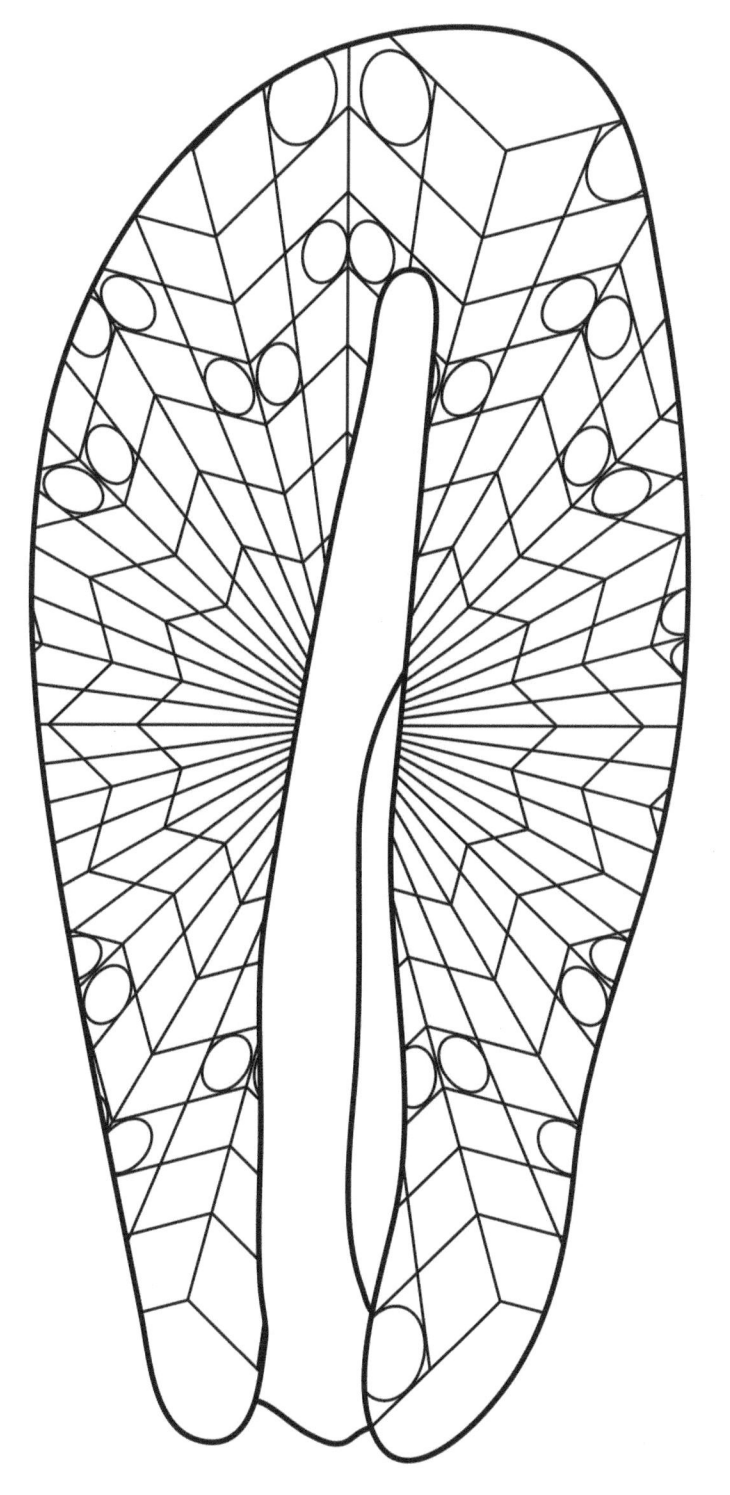

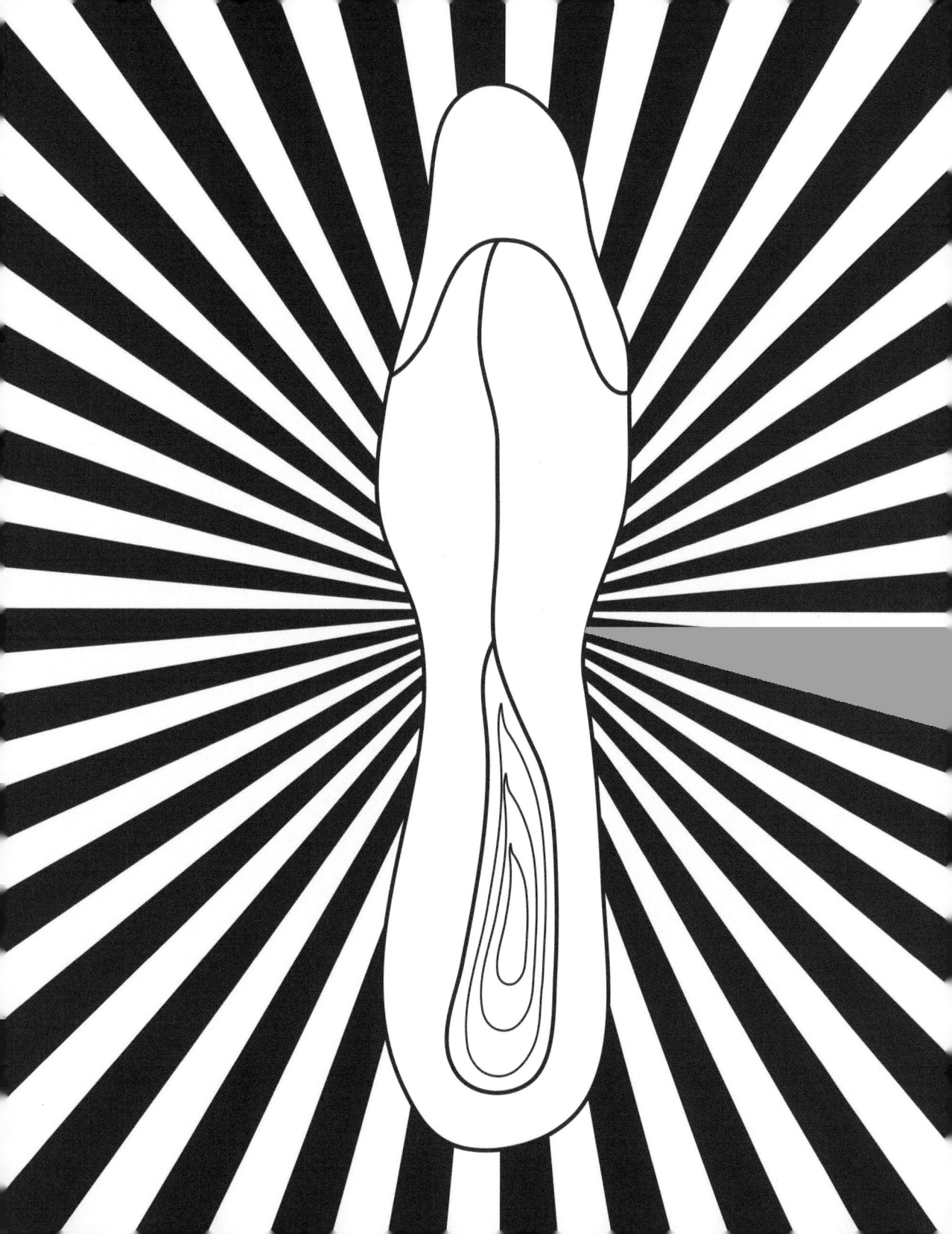

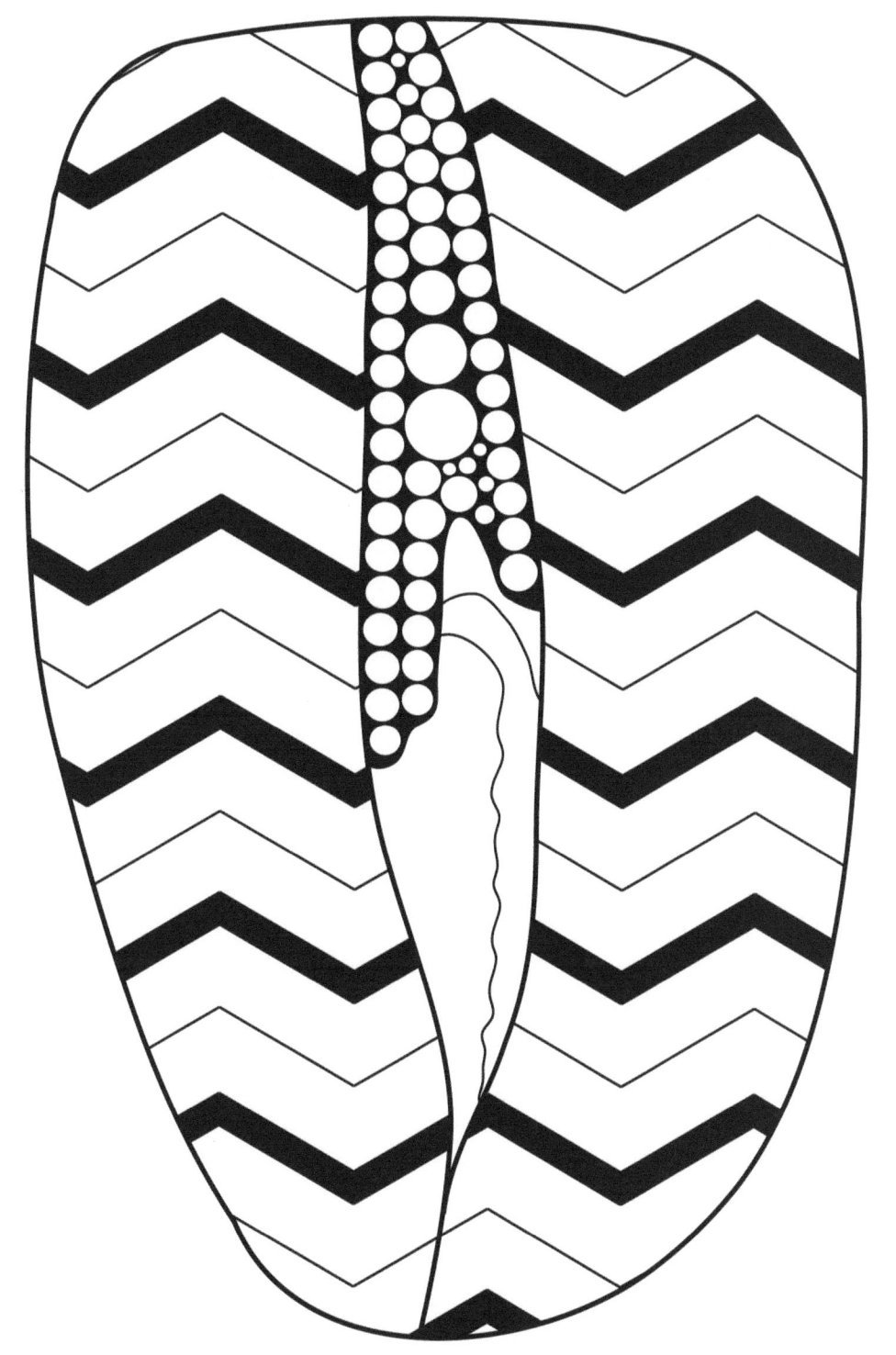

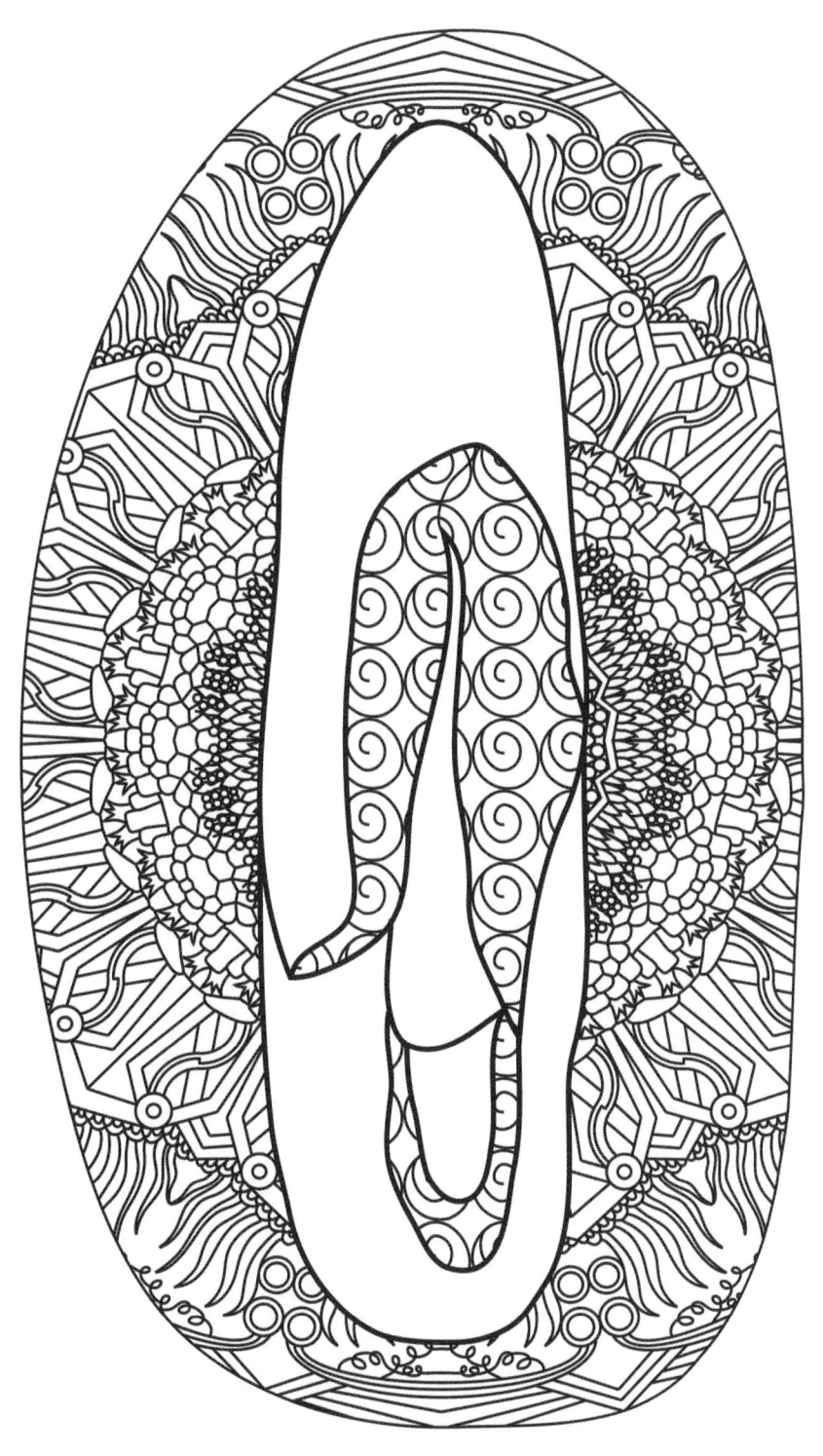

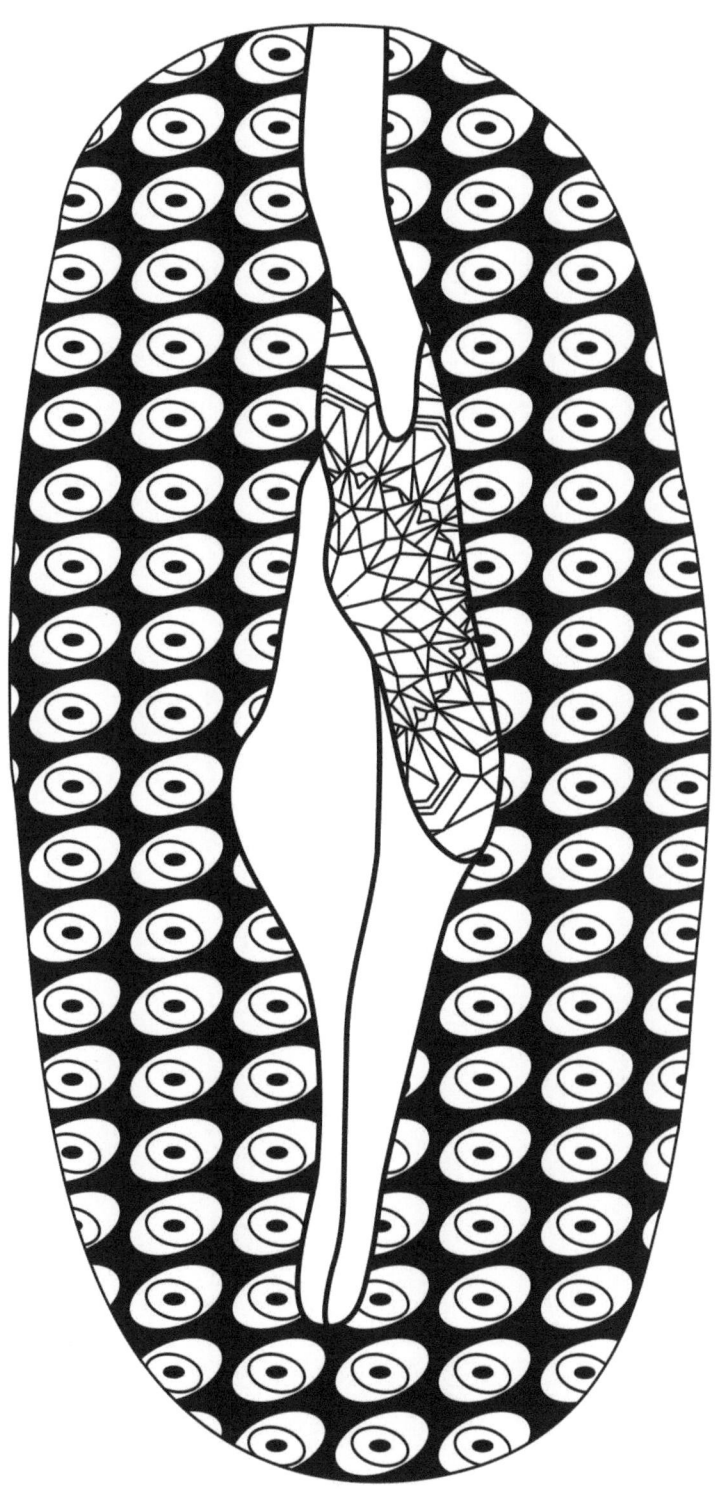

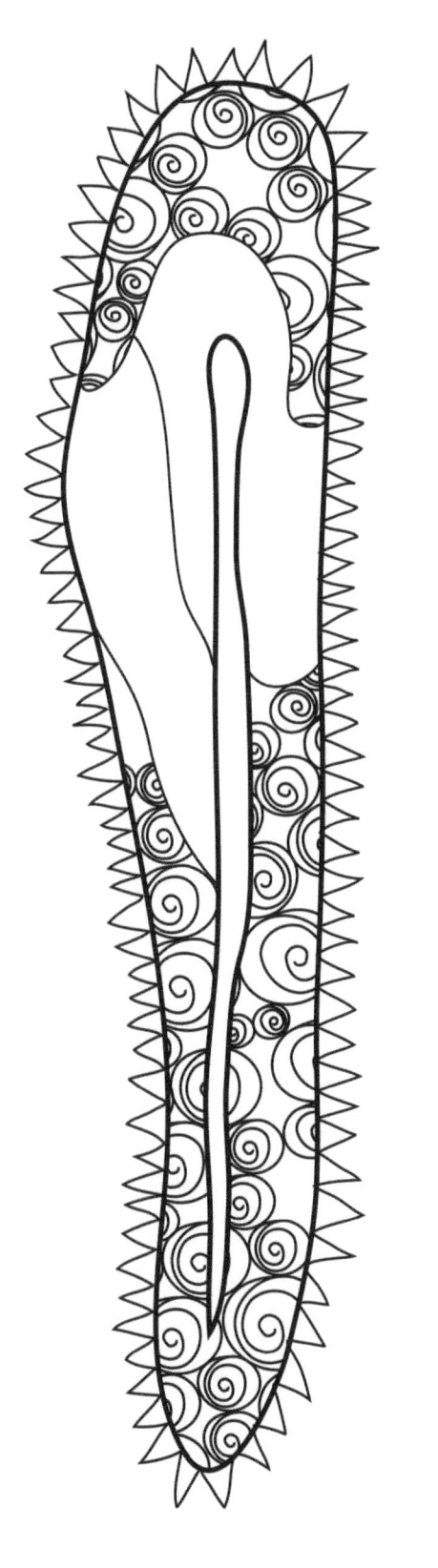

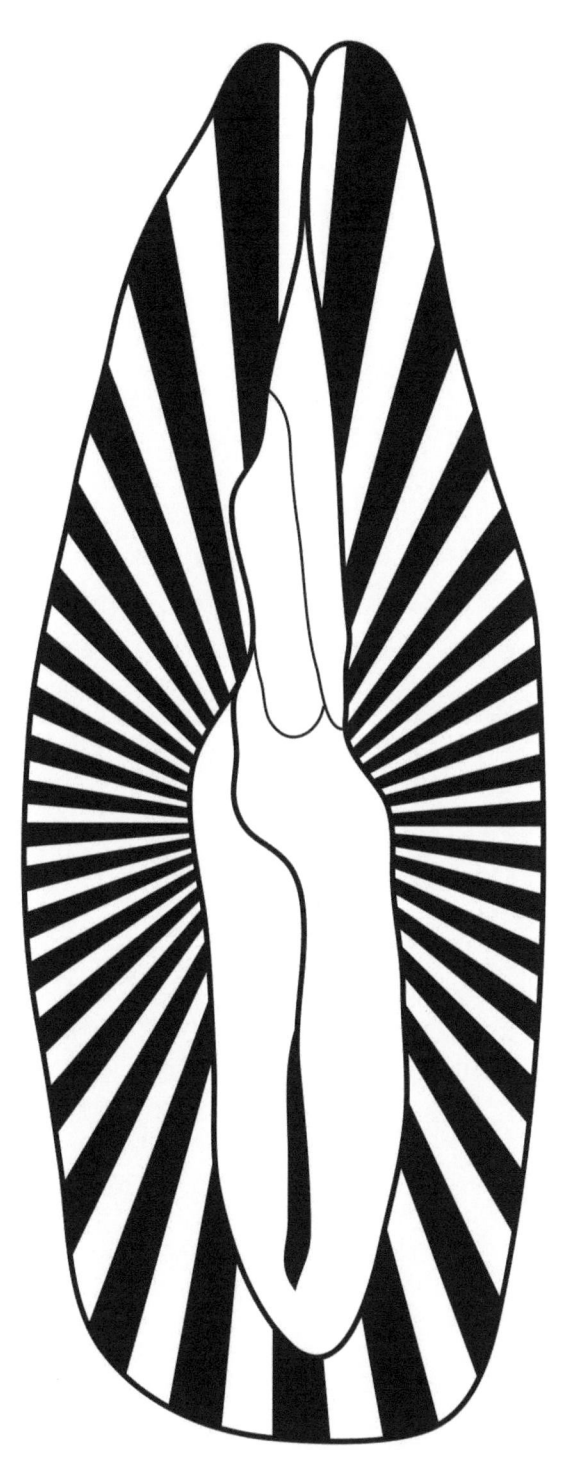

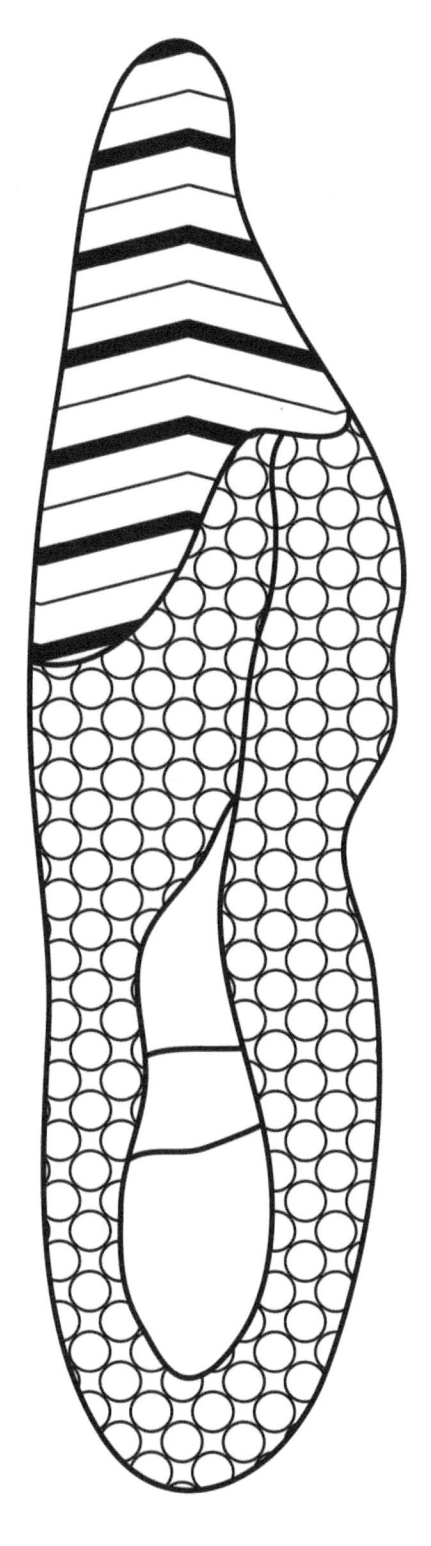

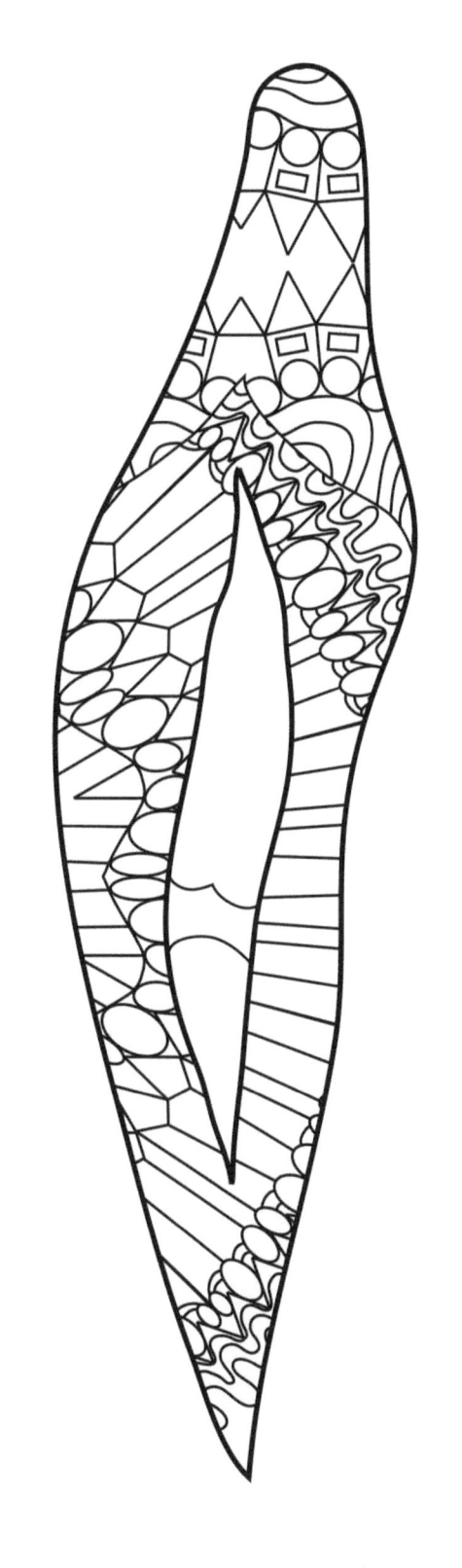

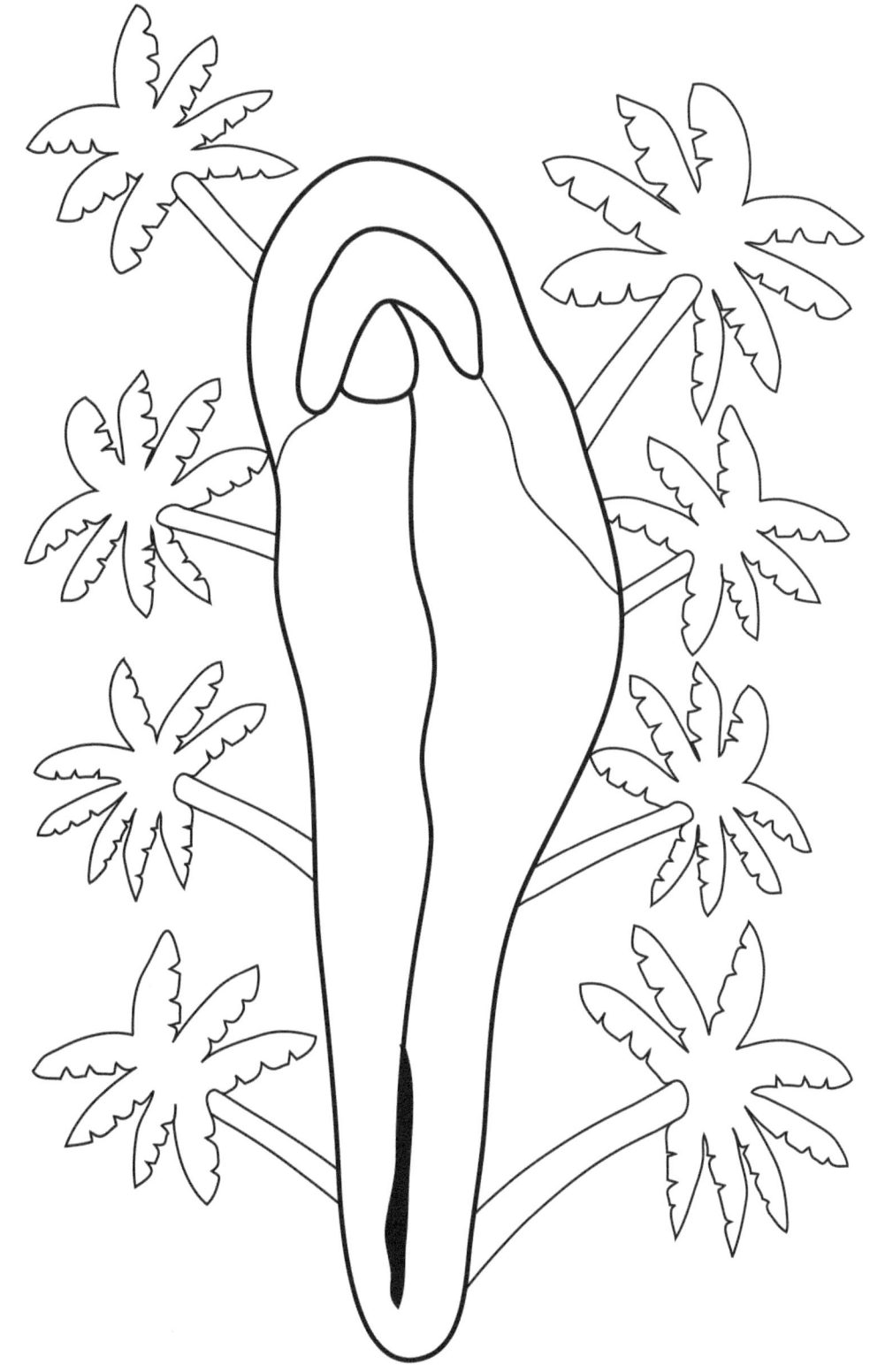

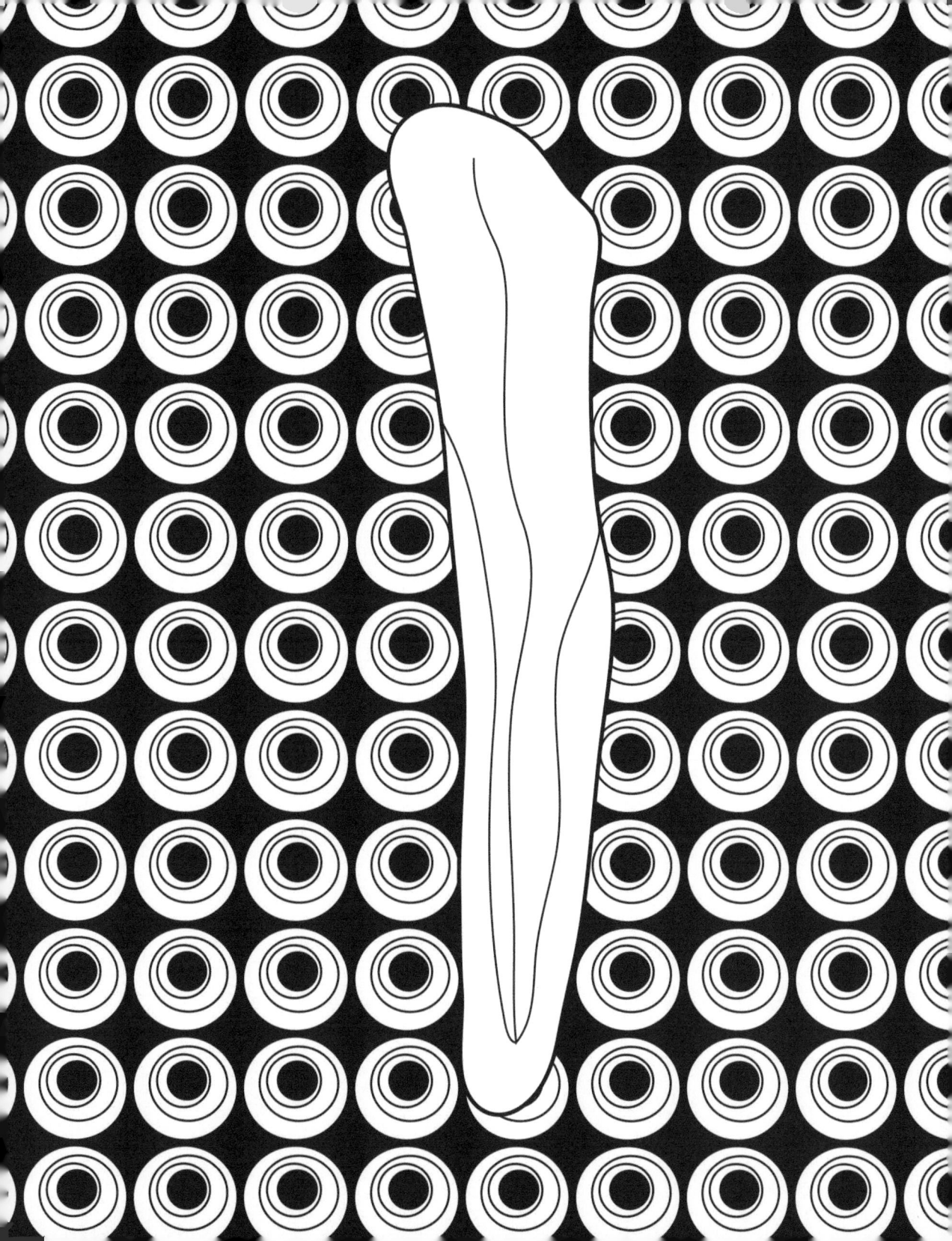